Baby Tips™
for new moms

5 to 8
Months

Baby Tips™
for new moms

5 to 8 Months

JEANNE MURPHY

FISHER BOOKS

Publishers: Bill Fisher
                      Helen V. Fisher
                      Howard W. Fisher

Managing Editor: Sarah Trotta

Cover Design: FifthStreet*design*, Berkeley, CA

Production: Deanie Wood
                      Randy Schultz
                      Josh Young

Cover Illustration: © 1998 Sharon Howard Constant

Illustrations: Cathie Lowmiller

Published by
Fisher Books
4239 W. Ina Road, Suite 101
Tucson, Arizona 85741
(520) 744-6110

To pass along your own helpful suggestions to
new mothers for future editions of this book,
please call (800) 617-4603.

Library of Congress Cataloging-in-Publication Data
Murphy, Jeanne, 1964-
  [Baby tips for new moms, 5 to 8 months]
  Jeanne Murphy's baby tips for new moms,
    5 to 8 months.
       p.   cm.
  Includes index.
  ISBN 1-55561-167-2
  1. Infants. 2. Infants—Care. 3. Infants—
    Development. 4. Mother and infant.
  HQ774.M888 1998
  649'. 122—dc21   98-16464
                                         CIP

Printed in the U.S.A.   Printing 5 4 3 2 1

Notice: The information in this book is true and complete to the best of our knowledge. It is
offered with no guarantees on the part of the author or Fisher Books. Author and publisher
disclaim all liability in connection with the use of this book.

The suggestions made in this book are opinions and are not meant to supersede a doctor's
recommendation in any way. Always consult your doctor before beginning any new program.

Contents

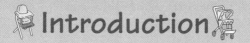 Introduction

Life is full of wonders
Both big ones and small.
You'll need a lifetime of learning
To appreciate them all.

These next few months will fly by as your baby grows from a 5-month-old to an 8-month-old. Baby is full of wonder and challenged to move.

It seems as though she will learn something new every day—from rolling over to picking up small objects with her fingers.

Encourage your child to try new things and to become confident and independent. Stifling a child won't change his personality, but it will frustrate him. Keep your little free spirit soaring!

Jeane

Fifth Month

If something in this book or any other book doesn't apply to your baby, don't panic. Remember, your baby is unique.

If you are planning an airplane trip, keep your child awake in the car on the way to the airport. For the sake of everyone else on the plane, don't let her fall asleep until you get on board.

Baby is probably trying to make his way around the crib now. Tuck in his blanket at the foot of the crib so he won't become tangled in it as he crawls forward.

To encourage your baby to try moving, put her favorite toys slightly out of reach.

Buy diapers, wipes and formula by the case. Your child will use these products for several more months.

Baby Tips

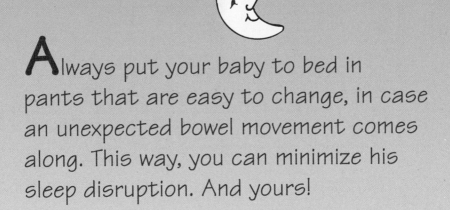

Always put your baby to bed in pants that are easy to change, in case an unexpected bowel movement comes along. This way, you can minimize his sleep disruption. And yours!

If your baby wakes up happy in the crib, let her stay there and play! This moment of contentment may give her time for a bowel movement, or she may fall back to sleep.

Don't panic if your child seems to be gagging on something. Give her a second to "cough it up" reflexively. (If your husband is panicking, gag **him**.)

If you need a baby-sitter for an extended period, try using two baby-sitters who split the work. This idea works especially well if you have a helpful family. Use your sitter for the first half and a family member for the second. The baby is kept busy, it's cheaper and no one becomes exhausted!

Baby powder is one of the best ways to cool down an irritable child. If you live in a warm climate, carry a bottle with you so you will always be ready if your baby becomes uncomfortable.

Another plus: It works just as well on you!

Keep a bottle of ipecac syrup on hand. Ipecac syrup induces vomiting.

Be aware that some things babies swallow **shouldn't** be vomited, but treated another way. At your baby's next appointment, talk to your doctor about the situations for which ipecac may be advised.

*O*at-ring cereals such as Cheerios®
are excellent starter foods because
they taste good and help develop
hand-mouth coordination. Many
studies have been done on these types
of foods for babies. Results have
shown oat-ring cereals are **great** for
babies, so use them confidently!

Did you know that at most stores, you can return or exchange unused diapers that are too small, and baby food and formula that is unopened? Just take them back to the store where you bought them. No questions asked.

Don't underestimate your child, even if he **is** a baby. For example, if your baby has accompanied you in the car on the same roads every day for a few months, believe me—he remembers the way and could probably teach **you**.

If your baby tries to roll over on her tummy whenever you begin to change her diaper, learn to put her diaper on backwards and you'll be set.

Baby Tips

Stop at the pet store! Your baby has been playing with stuffed animals for five months—he would probably love to meet a **real** one.

Show (and tell) your baby every day how much you love her.

Baby Tips

Invest your next couple of extra dollars in the greatest invention ever made for a mother . . . a remote-controlled car-starting device. With this gadget, you can start your car and warm it up on cold mornings from inside the house while you're still packing up the baby.

To learn your child's schedule, log his activities and bowel movements in a notebook or a personal computer over a 24-hour period. Add information to your notebook every day. Fill in some details, too, such as when he is alert or quiet. Post the schedule on your refrigerator and give your baby-sitter a copy.

Baby Tips

If you still can't find a schedule in your baby's day, create one! Start with meals served at the same time every day. Then add naps, bedtime and playtime . . . in that order.

Be quiet when your baby is trying to talk. He needs the chance to get a word in.

Learn what to do for your child if she chokes. Take a CPR class.

Don't worry—parents learn the words to most children's songs **without any help** by their baby's first birthday.

Your baby will perform random "mom checks." If he checks for you in the middle of the night, let him know you are near by patting his back, but avoid picking him up. (If you pick him up, he will remember his great success and try it again every night thereafter.)

While she's in the highchair, give your child a plastic, open cup with just a drop of liquid in it. Let her practice using it. Babies learn to drink from a cup amazingly fast. Covered "sippy cups" are great for certain things, but it helps to teach your child the right way the **first** time.

When you clean up a room, remember to roam the floor at baby's level. Pick up any small objects baby might be inclined to swallow. Look for rough or splintered places along the molding—sand and repaint those spots.

Secure everything in your house so nothing can be pulled over accidentally by small, exploring hands. Keep glass objects out of your baby's reach. Secure pole lamps or floor lamps. Baby might try to pull himself up and pull them over. If you can't secure an object, relocate it away from your baby for the time being.

The minute they can scoot or crawl, babies head for tablecloths (set for dinner), telephones and electrical cords. Minimize your baby's exposure to these potential hazards, too! And only use electrical-outlet covers that close automatically.

Separate different foods on your baby's plate as much as you can. This way, your child won't accidentally eat something she isn't expecting, especially while she is experimenting with new textures.

If you stay out late at night, don't forget you will be going back to work as soon as you get home (or you'll be on call, at least)!

Just because you don't understand what your baby is saying doesn't mean your baby doesn't understand what **you** are saying.

The expert about your child is not your doctor. It's you!

If you have a small family, but good friends, call them "aunt, uncle and cousin" for your child's sake.

Baby Tips

Sixth Month

If your baby leans toward you with an open mouth, he is probably hungry . . . but he may be trying to give you a kiss!

Some children never crawl. They go from sitting to standing to **running!**

Zinc oxide or Vaseline® petroleum jelly is used on diaper rash. These products create a barrier to protect the baby's skin from his diaper and bowel movements. They also soothe the skin and promote healing. If your child has diaper rash and diarrhea, be sure to use a barrier cream on his bottom.

Vaseline petroleum jelly is also a great barrier cream for the baby's face when you are introducing her to acidic foods, such as oranges and spaghetti sauce. (But be sure to keep it off your clothes.)

People were always telling me it would be "all over" once my child started crawling or walking. But life actually became easier at that point, because my son could get exactly what he wanted for himself. (More proof things tend to work out for the best!)

If you are having a bad day, expect baby to be having one, too.

Children love anything tiny, and they especially like to put those tiny things in their mouths. To prevent choking, make sure that anything near your baby is bigger than his fist.

Baby Tips

If you trust your baby-sitter, don't show up early more than once or twice, here and there.

If you have a good sitter and you arrive on time instead of early, you may not have to straighten up the house!

Once your baby establishes a morning wake-up schedule, she will probably be more reliable than your alarm clock.

Instead of feeding your child commercially prepared baby foods at every meal, put a combination of foods from your plate through the blender every now and then. You'll teach your baby to enjoy the same foods your family enjoys.

One of my best friends has a baby who insisted on a Caesar salad with dinner at least once a week after he turned two!

If you are concerned about leaving your fussy baby with your parents overnight, consider this: Babies are usually better-behaved with others than they are with their own parents. So go ahead, try it!

It may take your baby several years to learn to swim, so start early. Six months of age is a good time to start, but not before.

If your baby is a "whiner," you are probably responsible, unfortunately. To break her of this habit, have her spend more time with others. She may be whiny because she is too dependent on you.

Don't let your baby get in the habit of throwing food. If he doesn't eat, he's either not hungry or he doesn't like what you're serving. Either way, make sure you say "no" and then try feeding him the same food again a little later. You can only tell that babies don't like food when you know they are hungry.

The mother's rule of thumb for entertaining guests with children is to "clean up afterward, not before."

Baby Tips

If your baby is in a really bad mood, pretend he is a stressed-out grown-up caught in a rush-hour traffic jam. People can be really nasty in that kind of situation until you smile at them. But usually, once you do, they smile back—**and even wave!**

$\boldsymbol{B}$abies follow the philosophy, "Don't expect me to eat anything that you won't eat."

Don't leave your child with a person too old, too young or too dumb.

If the clock has changed because of daylight-savings time, the baby's schedule will change temporarily, too.

To maintain your child's interest in his toys, put away a few each time your child receives a new one. Bring them out again in six months.

If you want to get rid of some toys because you have too many, donate new or slightly used toys to local charities, schools, hospitals, places of worship and daycare centers.

If no one else is bringing children, don't bring yours.

Saltine and graham crackers dissolve easily and are great starter foods. But do not put them in a carry bag or a diaper bag unless they are in a hard container. They will break into a million pieces . . . which is why they are great starter foods!

If your baby is running on schedule, but won't take a nap, let her play naked for 15 minutes. That airs her out and makes her feel good. Afterward, dress her snugly, give her a warm bottle and try the nap again.

Baby Tips

It's OK to let your baby cry for a little while sometimes. Crying is actually good for babies. Some say it helps develop their lungs.

If your child isn't doing something another child his age is, don't panic. Write yourself a note and check it out at your next doctor visit. Your child may be doing something already that the other child isn't. Don't worry unless the doctor says to.

Babies love to watch their family members do **anything.** If you leave your child with a sitter, leave videotapes of your family, too. If the baby gets cranky, your sitter can play the tape, and voilá—instant comfort and familiarity! Just remember . . . probably the baby will be fine and the **sitter** will watch the tape.

I used to tease my sister that my niece "had a hollow leg" because she ate so much as a baby but never gained weight. My first baby was a "picker" and he was huge! Then I had my second child. My second baby eats like a horse but he too gains weight slowly. (Apparently my first one got **my** genes.) I now realize all babies really are different.

If your child falls down, don't assume she hurt herself. Check her over right away, but remember: Your reaction may have a greater effect on your baby than the accident itself.

Let your child be challenged. That's how he learns.

First haircuts are usually not a delightful experience, but they do become easier with time.

Don't be distressed if you notice your 6-month-old baby is wearing you out more than ever. You've been through six months of hormonal changes. In the meantime, your baby has enjoyed lots of sleep, a good diet and plenty of exercise. **He's** probably ready for the Junior Olympics!

Baby Tips

Seventh Month

Don't be afraid to say "no" to your baby, and start early.

Baby Tips

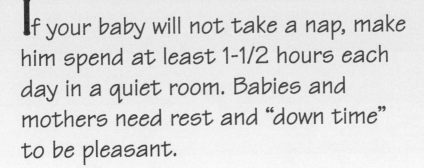

If your baby will not take a nap, make him spend at least 1-1/2 hours each day in a quiet room. Babies and mothers need rest and "down time" to be pleasant.

If anyone invites you to a gathering and uses the expression, "bringing your baby is up to you," immediately respond with, "Oh, we will definitely get a baby-sitter."

Baby Tips

Start taking your child to your house of worship early. This way, at an early age, he will learn about respect and how to be quiet.

If you haven't introduced foods yet, your baby is waiting. Remember, one food at a time in case of an allergic reaction.

Let's all get together and sign a petition for post offices to become drive-throughs.

Don't hesitate to buy low-cost alternatives for some baby items, especially medicines. Often they are made by the same manufacturer and are exactly the same product as the higher-priced, advertised brand.

If your baby wakes up in the night screaming, but does not open her eyes (as though she were still asleep), she may have a gas bubble. Try burping her or using a gas-relief product first. Don't immediately try to feed the baby; it could make her more miserable. And it may reverse all the progress you made in weaning her from night feedings.

Forgive yourself if you don't diagnose or notice something important about your baby. You are a mother, not a rocket scientist. (And if you are a rocket scientist, you are probably still not a general-practice physician, pediatrician, psychotherapist, psychologist, teacher, speech pathologist **and** pharmacist. And if you are, uh-oh!)

If your child won't try new foods or is a fussy eater, don't feed her too much formula during the day. Formula fills up your baby and makes it that much harder for you to get her to eat something different.

Don't let your child run the family. The father is the father. The mother is the mother, and the child is the child. And that's OK!

Babies need to develop independence. It is our job as parents to show them how. For example, show your baby how to hold his bottle so he can drink from it. Babies can pick up a trick like shaking a rattle in two seconds at around four months; believe me, at around seven months, they can hold up their own bottle and probably want to.

Make sure you've seen your baby smile at her caregiver at least once.

Try using a little cup, like the ones from children's medicine bottles, when making the transition from bottle to cup. They are small, hold a little bit of fluid and are fun for the baby to hold—just his size!

Also, put a plastic tablecloth underneath the highchair when you feed him. You'll save yourself a lot of needless scrubbing.

People blame a child's parents for the way she is. Worse, the child blames the parents for the way she is . . . later.

Baby Tips

Try not to run to the rescue every time your baby becomes frustrated or cries. Let him first try to work out his problems for himself. Your restraint, difficult though it may be, is especially important when you are helping your baby learn to sleep through the night.

*B*eware of the word "never." As in, "I will never take my child to a fast-food restaurant."

Let your child learn cause and effect. Let him explore under your watchful eye and play with lots of toys.

If you have a light-colored carpet in your baby or family room, and you see a busy-print carpet on sale anywhere, buy it and put it over your light carpet to protect it. Leave it there for a few years.

If your child is under two years old, keep a stroller, walking device and portable playpen in the car. (This will make your husband mad and your child happy, but that's generally the case!)

Be advised: If you attend a social event with a child under two years old, you will be spending your time in a quiet room, parking lot or park—not at the party.

If your child wants to get down and go when you are trying to hold him on your lap, save yourself a lot of trouble by letting him down to play. Don't be too apologetic. Other parents usually understand these things.

If your baby is due for a shot, try giving him his favorite toy about two minutes before the nurse gives the shot. Take it away just before the shot, and your baby will look to you for the toy. After the shot, when the baby starts to wail, smile and say,

"I'm sorry, honey," and give him back the toy. He will probably forget about the shot as soon as he gets his toy back. (And let me tell you, if a baby can forget about a shot that easily, he'll also forget that you had anything to do with it.)

If your child refuses to drink anything but juice, give her a serving of formula or expressed breast milk in a colorful "sippy cup" with a lid.

If you buy your child a ticket to any event, be sure the performance lasts no longer than three minutes.

Isn't it wonderful—when your baby is about to walk, many people will advise you to remove sharp-sided furniture, such as the coffee table, from your home. They say your child might hit his head on it if he loses his balance standing up those first wobbly times.

Bumping his head could make him hesitate to try standing and walking again (for a little while!).

However, just as many people will tell you to leave your furniture right where it is and let the baby get used to it. If you do leave your furniture in place, pad the sharp corners just to be safe.

If your child is home all day, take the time to put her in a position to see productive people doing productive things—starting with you! You are your baby's example, so be the best example you can be.

By the way, thank God for your baby!

Your child watches you every day. He wants to be just like you and do what you do. While he is watching you brush your teeth, dab his tongue every now and then with your family brand of toothpaste. He'll be familiar with the flavor and ready to go by the time his teeth come in.

If you want a good child, keep good children in her company . . . and remember the reverse.

When you can look deep into your child's eyes and know **he knows** exactly what he is doing, it's time to start setting rules.

Baby Tips

Eighth Month

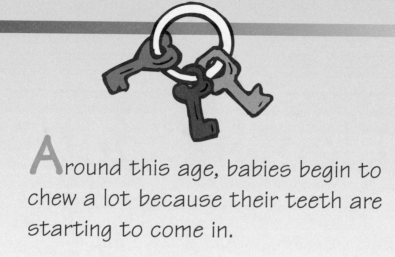

Around this age, babies begin to chew a lot because their teeth are starting to come in.

Chilled teething rings and biscuits come in handy. Two other great ideas are chilled oat rings and fruit from a baby jar.

An activity center in the crib is a great idea now because the baby will wake up and play with it instead of cry.

Baby Tips

Ear problems in babies are frequently caused when fluid builds up in the ear and becomes infected.

Try not to be overprotective. Most babies are naturally cautious, but keep an eye on them at all times, especially around a swimming pool. If you have a pool, a latched gate and a motion sensor are excellent ideas. A fence may be required by law.

If you drive by a park, stop in! Fresh air revitalizes you and the baby.

If you want to avoid having a family bed later, keep your baby in his own bedroom now, even if he wakes up in the middle of the night and you comfort him. Don't get into the habit of bringing your baby into your bed unless you want him to move in with you later on.

If you feel your child may have a learning disability, don't wait. Take your child to a specialist. Most parents of children with disabilities say they "had a feeling" long before it was confirmed.

A blistering diaper rash can be the result of a reaction to medicine.

Help your child learn to rely on herself.

If your child wakes up and wants to play with you at 1 a.m., don't do it! Teach your baby that if she wants to stay up alone, it's up to her—but **you** plan to get some sleep. Monitor her closely, but don't respond unless you are prepared to play with her every night at that time.

While you are naming pictures and reading to your child, don't forget to spell out some of the simple words.

When you sing "Twinkle, Twinkle, Little Star" to your child, use your fingers to twinkle!

Baby Tips

Go look for a frog or a lizard with your baby! You'll be glad you did when you see him belly laugh at the way those little critters jump or run.

Word to the wise: If it's an important day and the baby **must** look great, she will either scratch her face or get a bad haircut.

Lighten up! Do something silly, like a cartwheel, in front of your child. It will crack him up! (Just make sure it doesn't crack you up too!)

If you want to experience something wholly natural, watch the way your child climbs stairs.

Burn Watch: Once your baby starts to crawl, be sure she doesn't try to stand up by pulling on the stove (such as the oven door). Watch that she doesn't reach up to touch one of the heating elements or pull a pot off the stove. Don't let your baby play on or around your stove at all!

This goes for irons and ironing boards, too. Always put them away when you are done.

Your baby can become allergic to anything (for example, diapers and formula), even if he has used or eaten the same items before without a reaction. Babies may react to a change in laundry detergents, too.

If you use bad language around your baby, don't be surprised by his first words.

Don't give your child juice in the middle of the night. Besides not being good for her teeth, juice is mostly sugar and will wake her up.

Try not to argue with anyone, especially your spouse, in front of your child. You will see how much it upsets him, even at this early age. Teach your child to love and respect others by example.

If it is warm outside, let your baby play in a baby pool in the morning (or give your baby a bath in the morning instead of the evening). It makes her hungry, wears her out—and it's fun!

This is a real woman-to-woman tip . . . Whatever you do, **don't** tell your husband that you don't want anything for Christmas because you got the baby and that's enough, because it's the only thing he'll remember all year long.

Babies love sing-a-long videotapes and Richard Scarry's *Busy Town*™ series. Try them!

Baby Tips

Babies' fingernails and toenails are like razor blades when left uncut. If your baby screams and you don't know why, he may have scratched himself. Keep your baby's nails trimmed flush with the skin to prevent scratches.

Some doctors will never agree that your baby is teething, but mothers know better!

Baby Tips

Tell your husband that if he ever plans a surprise party for you, to make sure you are not carrying a sleeping baby through the door at the moment everyone yells "Surprise!" Otherwise, the party may be fun for everyone else, but it won't be for you.

If someone you trust wants to play with your baby, say, "Sure, take your time!"

Baby Tips

If you are letting your baby cry in her crib, listen carefully to make sure she doesn't throw up.

Most important, Mom, listen to your own internal "monitor" . . . Mothers know best!

Index

134

Enter the Baby Tips™ Contest.

Win more than $5,000 for your baby's education!

Share your special tip to soothe a cranky child, introduce her to the joys of spinach, or prepare him for a potty-training marathon. Come up with the first-prize-winning tip and receive a $5,000.00 educational bond plus hundreds of dollars' worth of baby accessories. Second- and third-place winners will receive an assortment of baby supplies.

Entries must be in the form of a "tip" or suggestion for parents with children age three or younger. Clearly print or type each suggested tip (no more than 75 words) on a 3 x 5 index card. Include your name, address, and daytime phone number. Only one entry per household, but each entry can include several tips.

The Baby Tips™ contest runs September 1, 1998, through January 31, 1999. The winner will be announced in March, 1999. All entries must be original tips created by the contestant. Purchase is not required. Entries will be judged by Fisher Books. All entries and their use become the property of Fisher Books.

Mail your entry to: Baby Tips™ Contest
　　　　　　　　　　4239 W. Ina Road #101
　　　　　　　　　　Tucson, AZ 85741

Toys and Activities for Young Children:

From birth to 3 months, children begin to smile at people and follow moving persons or objects with their eyes, they prefer faces and bright colors and will turn their head toward sounds.

To engage them in activities, they enjoy: rattles, large rings, squeeze or sucking toys, lullabies, bright pictures of faces, cardboard or vinyl books with high-contrast illustrations.

From 4 to 6 months, children prefer parents and older siblings to other people, will repeat actions that have interesting results, laugh, gurgle and imitate sounds.

They enjoy playing with soft dolls, socks with bright designs, toys that make noise when batted, squeezed or mouthed; fingerplays, simple songs and peek-a-boo.

From 7 to 12 months, they begin to explore, bang or shake objects with hands, identify themselves, body parts and voices of familiar people. They may become shy or upset with strangers.

They enjoy playing with wooden or soft plastic toy vehicles, large plastic balls, water toys that float, board books to read, puppets and tearing up old magazines.

Reprinted with permission from the brochure *TOYS: Tools for Learning,* available from the National Association for the Education of Young Children.

Resources for Parents

Asthma and Allergy Foundation
Consumer Information Line
1125 15th St. NW, Suite 502
Washington, DC 20005
800-7-ASTHMA
www.aafa.org
Provides information to parents of children
with asthma, reactive airway disease
or allergies.

American Academy of Pediatrics
141 Northwest Point Blvd.
Elk Grove Village, IL 60009-0927
847-228-5005
www.aap.org
Provides information and publishes free
brochures on children's health issues.

Cesarean Support, Education, and Concern
22 Forest Rd.
Framingham, MA 01701
508-877-8266
Call to receive local listings of Cesarean
support groups in your area.

International Parents Without Partners
800-637-7974
Offers education and referral services.
Organizes events for single parents.

La Leche League Hotline
800-LALECHE
847-519-7730
www.lalecheleague.org

Provides information and support to nursing
mothers.

**National Association for the Education
of Young Children**
1509 16th Street NW
Washington, DC 20036-1426
800-424-2460
www.naeyc.org

Call for brochures and catalog on
other areas of child development
and education.

National Association of Mothers Centers
64 Division Avenue
Levittown, NY 11756
800-645-3828
A national network of support and resource groups for mothers. Contact them to find your local support center for new parents—or help you start your own.

National Safe Kids Campaign
1301 Pennsylvania Ave. NW, Suite 1000
Washington, DC 20004
202-662-0600
www.safekids.org
Offers printed information on child safety, including fire safety and burn prevention. Seeks to raise public awareness of child injury prevention.

Nursing Mothers Counsel, Inc.
PO Box 500063
Palo Alto, CA 94303
408-272-1448
www.nursingmothers.org
Provides information and support to nursing mothers.

Postpartum Support, International
927 North Kellogg Ave.
Santa Barbara, CA 93111
805-967-7636
www.iup.edu/an/postpartum
Email: thonikman@compuserve.com
International network of concerned individuals and groups dedicated to increasing awareness about the emotional health of pregnant and postpartum women and their families.

US Consumer Product Safety Commission
Washington, DC 20207
800-638-2772

CareGuide – The Online Resource for Finding Childcare

Your childcare solution is only a click away!

CareGuide is an easy to use, interactive reference guide of childcare, preschools and day-care providers nationwide. To use, simply follow three steps: Go online to www.careguide.net, click on the "Search for Child Care" button and select your search criteria, then review the list of providers that match your needs. The comprehensive CareGuide listing contains facility-specific information such as: hours of operation, staff-to-child ratio, admission requirements, staff tenure and activities.

With this offer, an experienced CareGuide Referral Specialist will assist you in finding care FREE OF CHARGE. To contact a Referral Specialist, either fill out the form on our home site at www.careguide.net or call toll-free 1-888-389-8839.

Contact Information:
Web site address: www.careguide.net
E-mail address: care@careguide.net
Toll-Free Phone: 1-888-389-8839

PERFECTLY SAFE CATALOG

Keeping children safe is always a major concern for parents. With products from the Perfectly Safe catalog, every room in your home can be made safe. In addition, this catalog provides other useful products for traveling, on-the-go, in the car, and when your child is playing outdoors.

Whether you are looking for a bicycle helmet, a jogging stroller, a sinkadink (a small sink that fits over any standard bathtub) or a device to keep little ones from inserting their grilled cheese sandwich into your VCR, the Perfectly Safe catalog has what you need.

All Perfectly Safe products are tested and approved by families like yours.

To receive your free catalog, call 1-800-837-KIDS from anywhere in the US or Canada, or write:

The Perfectly Safe Catalog
7835 Freedom Ave. NW, Suite 3
North Canton, OH 44720-6907

PFIS98

Natural Baby Catalog

For the best in all-natural fabrics and materials, child-tested and parent-approved products, look into the Natural Baby Catalog. Specializing in products that emphasize health or comfort, this catalog offers everything from clothing to crib shoes, mocs to natural wooden toys, slides, rocking horses, cotton diapers and much more.

Many products are made of organically grown materials, and many of the companies are home businesses.

To receive a free copy of The Natural Baby Catalog, call 1-800-388-BABY, or write:

Natural Baby Catalog
7835 Freedom Ave. NW, Suite 2
North Canton, OH 44720-6907

NFIS98

Jeannie's Kid's Club

Want to save money while getting sensible products that will stimulate your child's imagination? Join Jeannie's Kid's Club and save hundreds of dollars on items for the nursery, toys for infants and toddlers, kids furniture and many other products.

If you join Jeannie's Kid's Club you can save up to 40% or more on many items, such as the Bedside Co-sleeper™, a clothing personalizer, pre- & post-natal stretch sleep bras, Comfort Temp™ thermometer, toys and much, much more.

Enjoy a 3-month trial membership for only $3.00!

Call 1-800-363-0500 to find out about Jeannie's Kid's Club, or write:

Kid's Club
7835 Freedom Ave NW, Suite 3
North Canton, OH 44720-6907

KFIS98

Breastfeeding Naturally

Receive a $1.50 rebate on this Fisher Books title. To receive your rebate, please follow these steps:

1. Purchase *Breastfeeding Naturally* pictured on front.

2. Mail original dated sales receipt and this coupon to:
   FIBO/Universal
   PO Box 222510
   Hollywood, FL 33022-2510

Name_____

Address_____

City, State, ZIP_____

Store where purchased_____

Rebate requests must be postmarked by Dec. 31, 1999. Please allow 4-6 weeks for receipt of rebate. All requests must use original rebate form and sales receipt. Copies or facsimiles will not be accepted.

BFN

Breastfeeding Your Baby

Receive a $1.50 rebate on this Fisher Books title. To receive your rebate, please follow these steps:

1. Purchase *Breastfeeding Your Baby* pictured on front.

2. Mail original dated sales receipt and this coupon to:
   FIBO/Universal
   PO Box 222510
   Hollywood, FL 33022-2510

Name_____

Address_____

City, State, ZIP_____

Store where purchased_____

Rebate requests must be postmarked by Dec. 31, 1999. Please allow 4-6 weeks for receipt of rebate. All requests must use original rebate form and sales receipt. Copies or facsimiles will not be accepted.

BYB

Your Pregnancy Week by Week

Receive a $1.50 rebate on this Fisher Books title. To receive your rebate, please follow these steps:

1. Purchase *Your Pregnancy Week by Week* pictured on front.

2. Mail original dated sales receipt and this coupon to:
   FIBO/Universal
   PO Box 222510
   Hollywood, FL 33022-2510

Name_____

Address_____

City, State, ZIP_____

Store where purchased_____

Rebate requests must be postmarked by Dec. 31, 1999. Please allow 4-6 weeks for receipt of rebate. All requests must use original rebate form and sales receipt. Copies or facsimiles will not be accepted.

YPW

Your Newborn & You

Receive a $1.50 rebate on this Fisher Books title. To receive your rebate, please follow these steps:

1. Purchase *Your Newborn & You* pictured on front.

2. Mail original dated sales receipt and this coupon to:
   FIBO/Universal
   PO Box 222510
   Hollywood, FL 33022-2510

Name_____

Address_____

City, State, ZIP_____

Store where purchased_____

Rebate requests must be postmarked by Dec. 31, 1999. Please allow 4-6 weeks for receipt of rebate. All requests must use original rebate form and sales receipt. Copies or facsimiles will not be accepted.

YNY

Your Baby & Your Work

Receive a $1.50 rebate on this Fisher Books title. To receive your rebate, please follow these steps:

1. Purchase *Your Baby & Your Work* pictured on front.

2. Mail original dated sales receipt and this coupon to:
   FIBO/Universal
   PO Box 222510
   Hollywood, FL 33022-2510

Name_____

Address_____

City, State, ZIP_____

Store where purchased_____

Rebate requests must be postmarked by Dec. 31, 1999. Please allow 4-6 weeks for receipt of rebate. All requests must use original rebate form and sales receipt. Copies or facsimiles will not be accepted.

YBW

Your Baby from Birth to 18 Months

Receive a $2.00 rebate on this Fisher Books title. To receive your rebate, please follow these steps:

1. Purchase *Your Baby from Birth to 18 Months* pictured on front.

2. Mail original dated sales receipt and this coupon to:
   FIBO/Universal
   PO Box 222510
   Hollywood, FL 33022-2510

Name_____

Address_____

City, State, ZIP_____

Store where purchased_____

Rebate requests must be postmarked by Dec. 31, 1999. Please allow 4-6 weeks for receipt of rebate. All requests must use original rebate form and sales receipt. Copies or facsimiles will not be accepted.

YBB

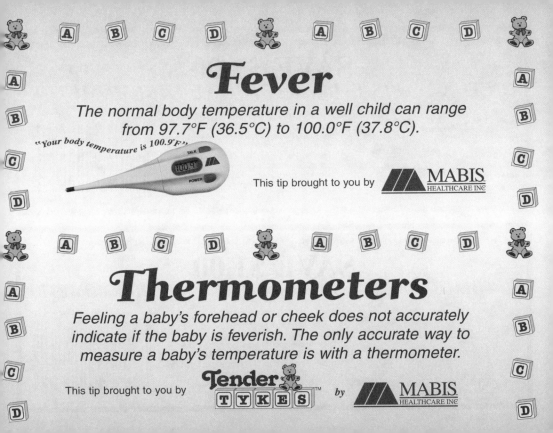

Fever

The normal body temperature in a well child can range from 97.7°F (36.5°C) to 100.0°F (37.8°C).

"Your body temperature is 100.9°F"

This tip brought to you by MABIS HEALTHCARE INC

Thermometers

Feeling a baby's forehead or cheek does not accurately indicate if the baby is feverish. The only accurate way to measure a baby's temperature is with a thermometer.

This tip brought to you by **Tender TYKES™** *by* MABIS HEALTHCARE INC

$5 REBATE ON ARRIVA® OR TURNABOUT® INFANT CAR SEAT

To receive your $5 rebate, follow these steps:

- Buy any Cosco Arriva or Turnabout Infant Car Seat and cut out the UPC (bar code symbol) from the carton.

- Mail this form, the UPC and your original dated sales receipt to:

**Cosco Promotion Fulfillment Dept. 069
P.O. Box 2609, Columbus, IN 47202-2609 USA**

Name_____

Address _____

City_____ State_____

Zip_____ Tel (   ) _____

Rebate requests must be postmarked by December 31, 2000. Please allow 4 to 6 weeks for receipt of rebate. Limit of one rebate per purchase. Cannot be combined with any other Cosco offer. Must be accompanied by original claim form and sales receipt (facsimiles will not be accepted). Void where prohibited.

$5 REBATE ON ROCK 'N ROLLER® STROLLER

To receive your $5 rebate, follow these steps:

- Buy any Cosco Rock 'n Roller Stroller and cut out the UPC (bar code symbol) from the carton.

- Mail this form, the UPC and your original dated sales receipt to:

**Cosco Promotion Fulfillment Dept. 069
P.O. Box 2609, Columbus, IN 47202-2609 USA**

Name_____

Address _____

City_____ State_____

Zip_____ Tel (   ) _____

Rebate requests must be postmarked by December 31, 2000. Please allow 4 to 6 weeks for receipt of rebate. Limit of one rebate per purchase. Cannot be combined with any other Cosco offer. Must be accompanied by original claim form and sales receipt (facsimiles will not be accepted). Void where prohibited.

$5 REBATE ON AN OPTIONS™ OR RISE & DINE™ HIGH CHAIR

To receive your $5 rebate, follow these steps:

- Buy any Cosco Options or Rise & Dine High Chair and cut out the UPC (bar code symbol) from the carton.

- Mail this form, the UPC and your original dated sales receipt to:

Cosco Promotion Fulfillment Dept. 069
P.O. Box 2609, Columbus, IN 47202-2609 USA

Name_____

Address _____

City_____ State_____

Zip_____ Tel ( ) _____

Rebate requests must be postmarked by December 31, 2000. Please allow 4 to 6 weeks for receipt of rebate. Limit of one rebate per purchase. Cannot be combined with any other Cosco offer. Must be accompanied by original claim form and sales receipt (facsimiles will not be accepted). Void where prohibited.

$5 REBATE ON TOURIVA®, REGAL RIDE™ OR OLYMPIAN™ CONVERTIBLE CAR SEAT

To receive your $5 rebate, follow these steps:

- Buy any Cosco Touriva, Regal Ride or Olympian Car Seat and cut out the UPC (bar code symbol) from the carton.

- Mail this form, the UPC and your original dated sales receipt to:

Cosco Promotion Fulfillment Dept. 069
P.O. Box 2609, Columbus, IN 47202-2609 USA

Name_____

Address _____

City_____ State_____

Zip_____ Tel ( ) _____

Rebate requests must be postmarked by December 31, 2000. Please allow 4 to 6 weeks for receipt of rebate. Limit of one rebate per purchase. Cannot be combined with any other Cosco offer. Must be accompanied by original claim form and sales receipt (facsimiles will not be accepted). Void where prohibited.